Facts About the Red Kite

By Lisa Strattin

© 2023 Lisa Strattin

FREE BOOK

FREE FOR ALL SUBSCRIBERS

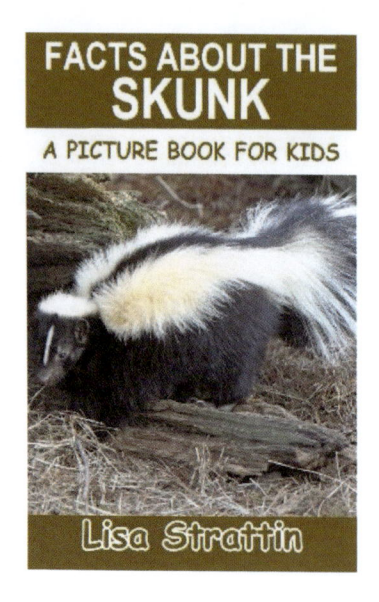

FACTS ABOUT THE SKUNK
A PICTURE BOOK FOR KIDS

Lisa Strattin

LisaStrattin.com/Subscribe-Here

BOX SET

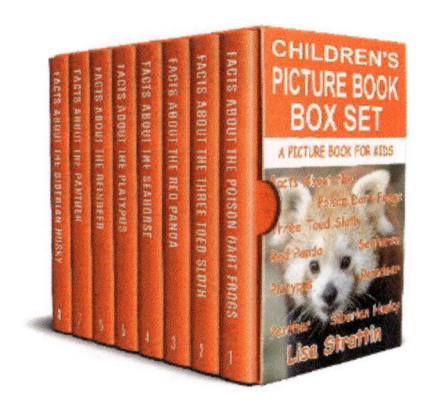

- **FACTS ABOUT THE POISON DART FROGS**
- **FACTS ABOUT THE THREE TOED SLOTH**
  - **FACTS ABOUT THE RED PANDA**
  - **FACTS ABOUT THE SEAHORSE**
  - **FACTS ABOUT THE PLATYPUS**
  - **FACTS ABOUT THE REINDEER**
  - **FACTS ABOUT THE PANTHER**
- **FACTS ABOUT THE SIBERIAN HUSKY**

LisaStrattin.com/BookBundle

Facts for Kids Picture Books by Lisa Strattin

Little Blue Penguin, Vol 92

Chipmunk, Vol 5

Frilled Lizard, Vol 39

Blue and Gold Macaw, Vol 13

Poison Dart Frogs, Vol 50

Blue Tarantula, Vol 115

African Elephants, Vol 8

Amur Leopard, Vol 89

Sabre Tooth Tiger, Vol 167

Baboon, Vol 174

Sign Up for New Release Emails Here

LisaStrattin.com/subscribe-here

All rights reserved. No part of this book may be reproduced by any means whatsoever without the written permission from the author, except brief portions quoted for purpose of review.

All information in this book has been carefully researched and checked for factual accuracy. However, the author and publisher makes no warranty, express or implied, that the information contained herein is appropriate for every individual, situation or purpose and assume no responsibility for errors or omissions. The reader assumes the risk and full responsibility for all actions, and the author will not be held responsible for any loss or damage, whether consequential, incidental, special or otherwise, that may result from the information presented in this book.

All images are free for use or purchased from stock photo sites or royalty free for commercial use.

Some coloring pages might be of the general species due to lack of available images.

I have relied on my own observations as well as many different sources for this book and I have done my best to check facts and give credit where it is due. In the event that any material is used without proper permission, please contact me so that the oversight can be corrected.

COVER IMAGE

https://www.flickr.com/photos/andymorffew/51210126263/

ADDITIONAL IMAGES

https://www.flickr.com/photos/hisgett/5939886462/

https://www.flickr.com/photos/24874528@N04/36208443646/

https://www.flickr.com/photos/29237715@N05/5777488226/

https://www.flickr.com/photos/sussexbirder/8066797939/

https://www.flickr.com/photos/alanshearman001/53102066816/

https://www.flickr.com/photos/davidpacey1975/16069875312/

https://www.flickr.com/photos/davidpacey1975/15450907933/

https://www.flickr.com/photos/hisgett/5939313937/

https://www.flickr.com/photos/davidpacey1975/13764296634/

https://www.flickr.com/photos/11152520@N03/2321869254/

Contents

INTRODUCTION 9

CHARACTERISTICS 11

APPEARANCE 13

LIFE STAGES 15

LIFE SPAN 17

SIZE 19

HABITAT 21

DIET 23

FRIENDS AND ENEMIES 25

SUITABILITY AS PETS 27

INTRODUCTION

The Red Kite is no ordinary bird; it's a special kind known as a bird of prey. These birds are like nature's very own superheroes, and the Red Kite is one of the coolest among them. With its wings spread wide and a keen eye for spotting prey, it soars high in the sky, showing off its incredible hunting skills.

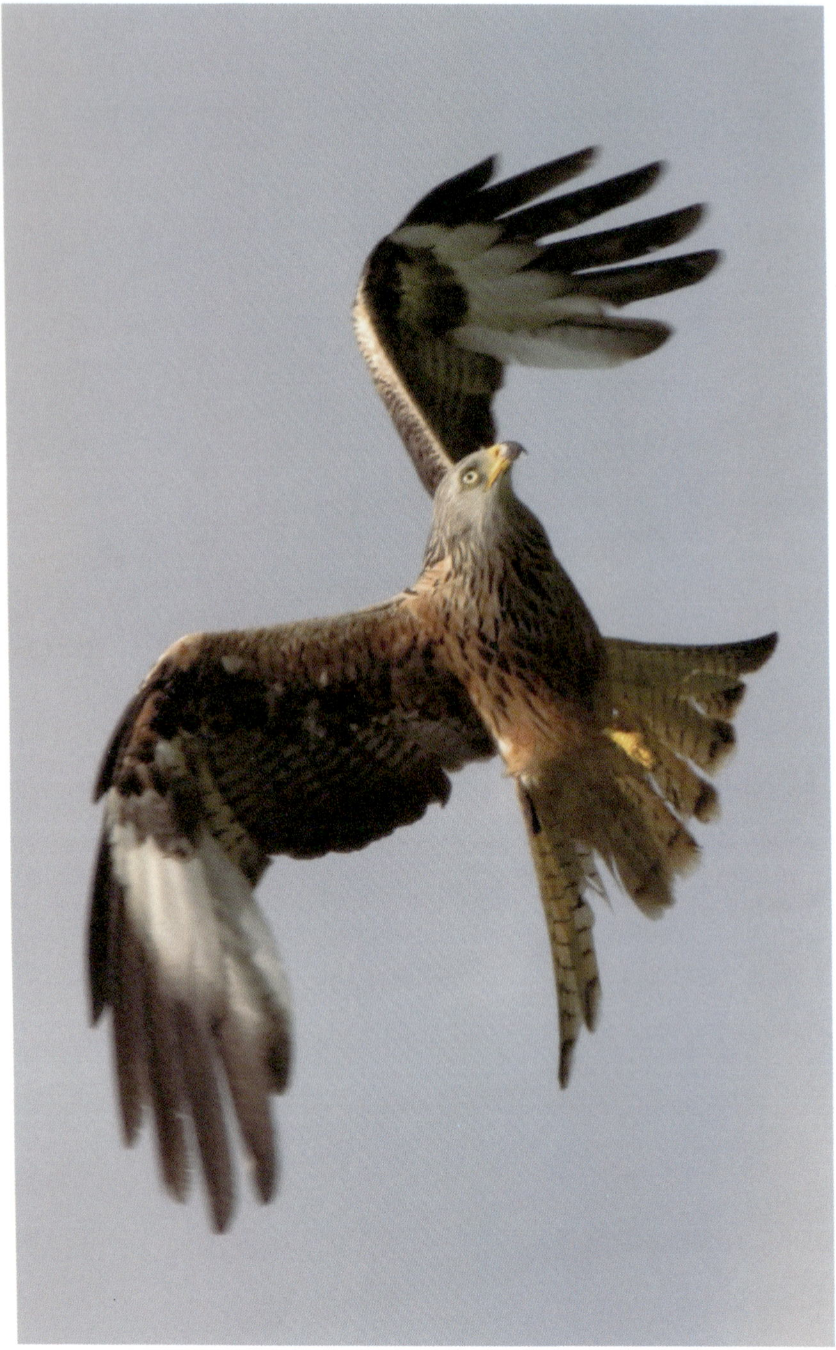

CHARACTERISTICS

The Red Kite is truly a remarkable bird with some unique characteristics that make it stand out in the avian world.

Majestic Wingspan: One of the most striking features of the Red Kite is its impressive wingspan. When it spreads its wings, they can reach up to 5.5 feet! That's even bigger than some grown-ups' arms!

Beautiful Colors: Red Kites are known for their stunning colors. They have deep reddish-brown feathers on their bodies, which contrast beautifully with their white heads. These colors make them easy to spot when they're soaring high in the sky.

Keen Eyes: Red Kites have incredibly sharp eyesight. They can spot small creatures from way up high in the sky, making them excellent hunters.

Impressive Soaring: These birds are masters of the sky! They love to glide and soar effortlessly, riding on air currents. It's like they're dancing with the wind!

Social Birds: Red Kites are often seen in groups, which makes them social birds. They like to hang out with their fellow Red Kites, and sometimes, they even share their meals.

Mysterious Meowing: If you ever hear a Red Kite up in the air, it might sound like it's meowing, almost like a cat! This unique sound is one way they communicate with each other.

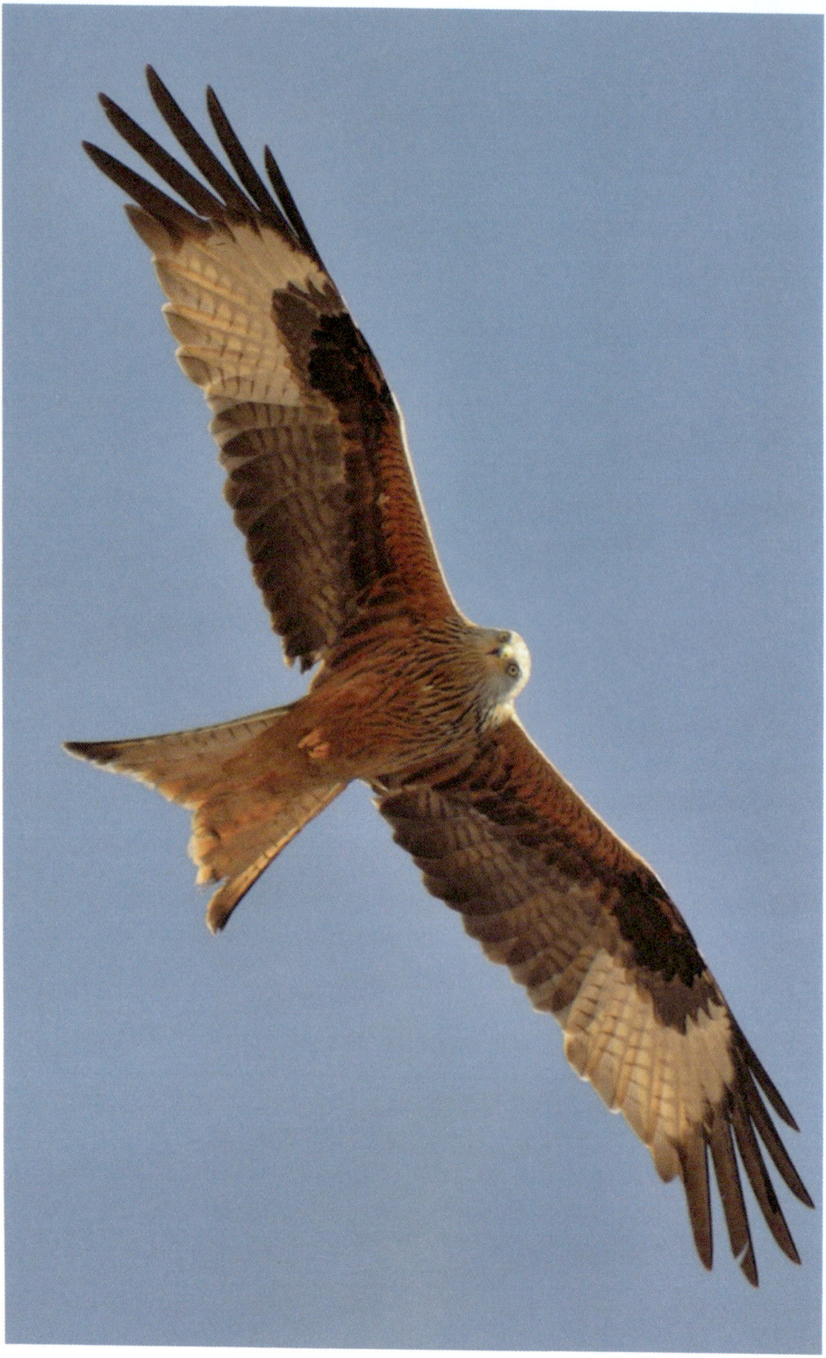

APPEARANCE

The Red Kite is a bird with a truly remarkable appearance that's sure to capture your imagination.

Feathers Like a Work of Art: If you spot a Red Kite soaring through the sky, you'll notice its feathers are like a beautiful painting. Their bodies are covered in rich reddish-brown feathers, and their heads are a crisp, snowy white. This striking color combination makes them easy to recognize.

Wings Wide Open: When the Red Kite spreads its wings, it's a sight to behold. Their wings are wide and strong, allowing them to glide gracefully through the air. These majestic birds are like aerial acrobats, showing off their incredible flying skills.

A Forked Tail: Look closely at the Red Kite's tail, and you'll see that it's split in two, like a pair of scissors. This unique tail shape helps them steer and balance while they soar through the skies.

Sharp Beak and Talons: Red Kites have sharp beaks and strong talons (claws) that are perfect for catching their prey. These tools are like their own special hunting equipment.

Sleek and Elegant: With their sleek bodies and elegant posture, Red Kites are the picture of grace in the bird world. They move with a certain dignity, whether they're perched on a tree branch or gliding high above.

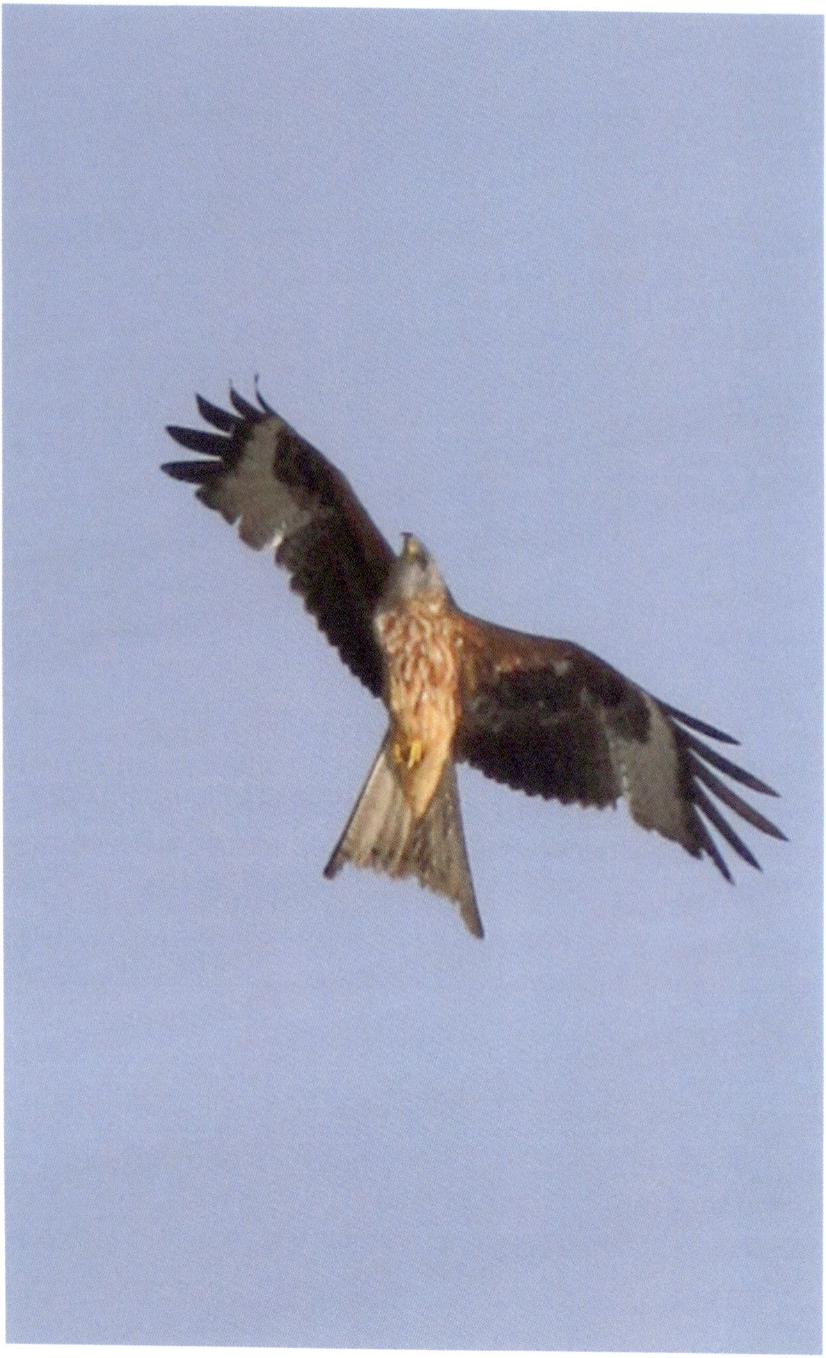

LIFE STAGES

The life of a Red Kite is like a fascinating story with different chapters. Let's explore the life stages of these incredible birds!

Egg Stage: It all begins with an egg! Red Kites start their lives as tiny eggs, usually laid in nests high up in trees. The parent birds take good care of these eggs, keeping them warm and safe until they hatch.

Hatchling Stage: After some time, the eggs crack open, and baby Red Kites, called hatchlings, emerge. At this stage, they're very small and covered in soft down feathers. They rely entirely on their parents for food and protection.

Fledgling Stage: As the young Red Kites grow, they go through a stage called fledging. During this time, they begin to practice flying. You can imagine them as little birdy beginners, flapping their wings and hopping around the nest.

Juvenile Stage: After they've learned to fly, the young Red Kites are called juveniles. They still depend on their parents but start exploring the world on their own. Their feathers begin to change, becoming more like those of adult Red Kites.

Adult Stage: Finally, the Red Kites become adults. Their feathers take on the beautiful colors we mentioned earlier, with reddish-brown bodies and white heads. They are now skilled hunters, finding their own food and even raising their own young.

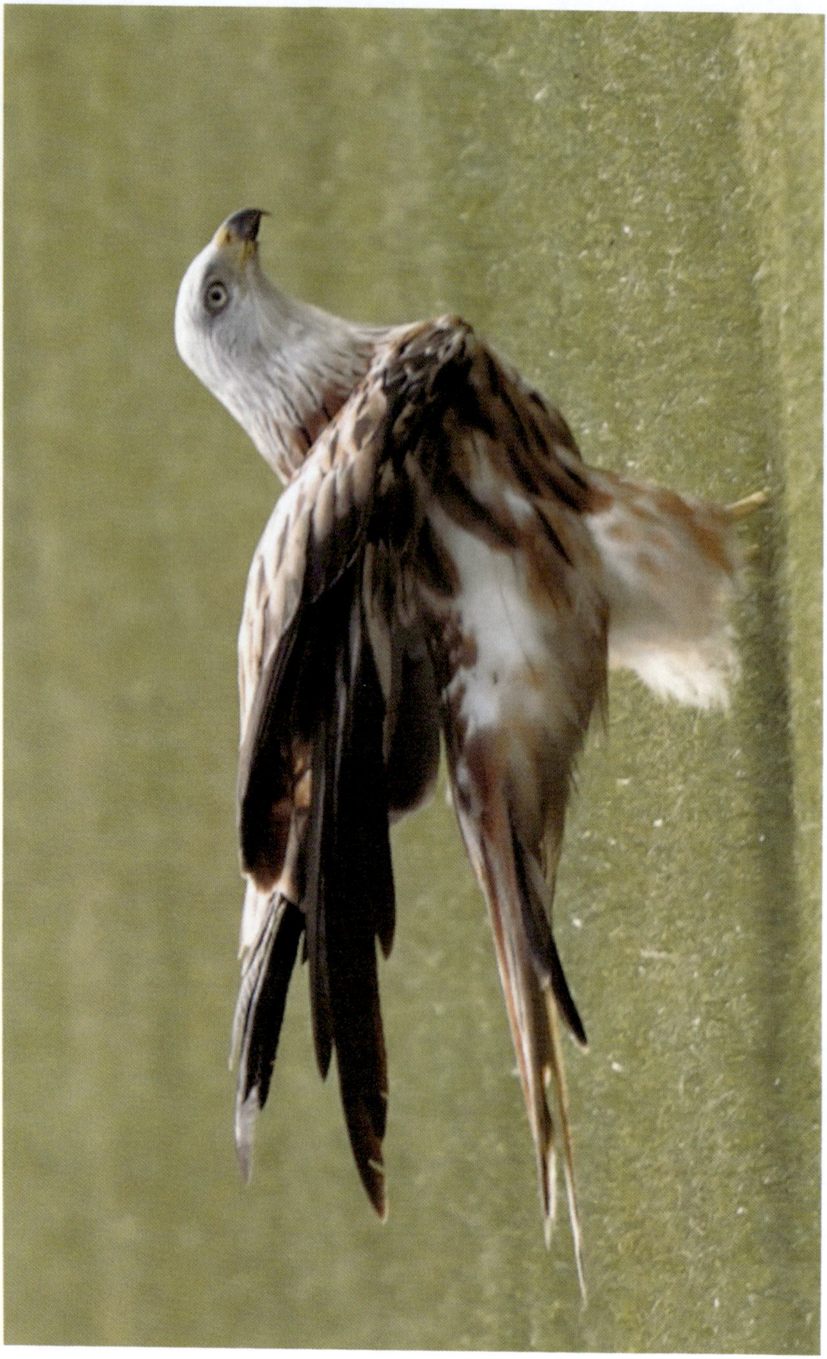

LIFE SPAN

The Red Kite's life span is like a journey that lasts for many years. These amazing birds can live for a long time, often reaching up to 15 to 20 years or even more! That's quite a lot of birthdays for a bird.

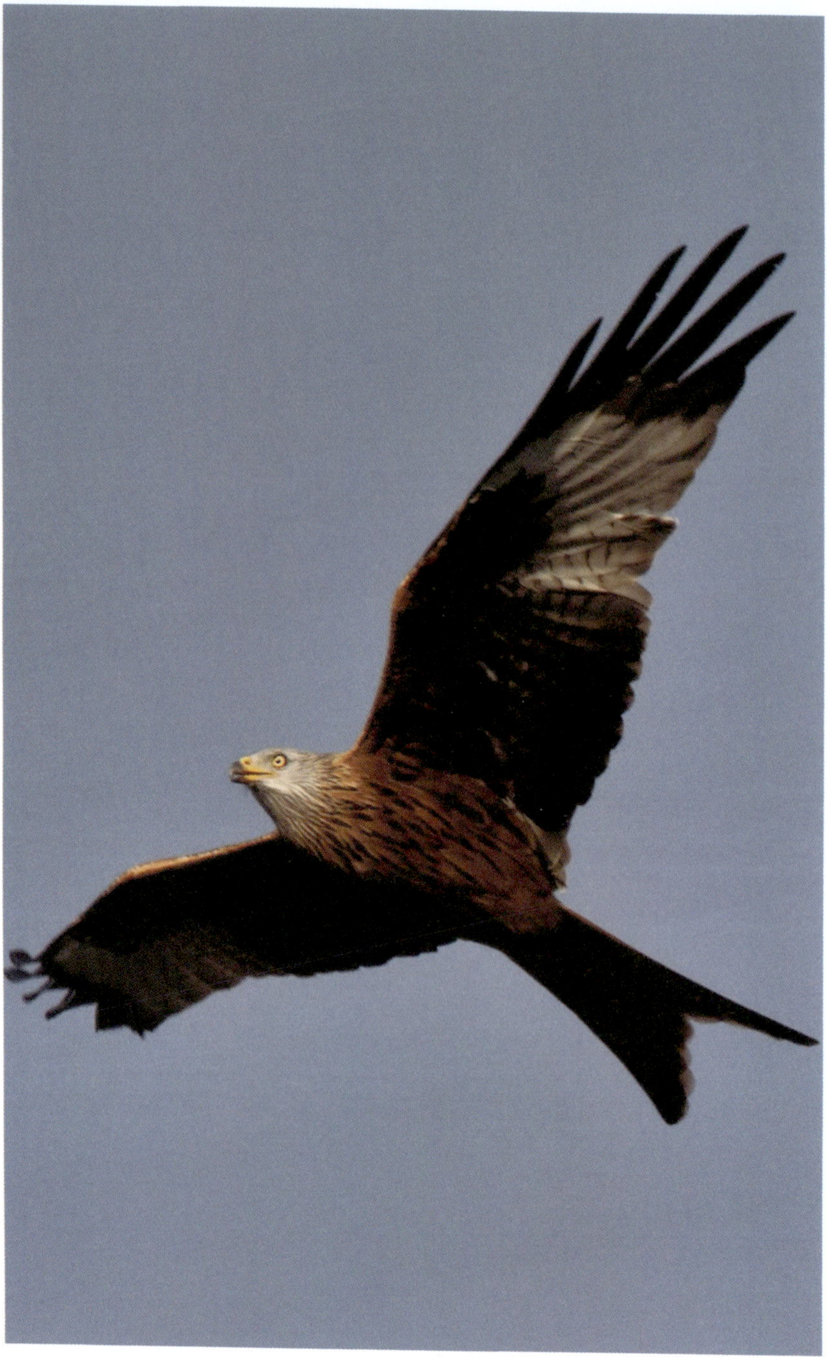

SIZE

The Red Kite is a bird that's just the right size for flying gracefully through the sky. It's not too big, like an eagle, and not too small, like a sparrow. You can think of it as being somewhere in the middle. When it stretches its wings wide, they look pretty impressive, but not gigantic.

Imagine if you could spread your arms out wide, and the tip of one hand could almost touch the tip of the other hand. That's kind of like how wide a Red Kite's wings can be. And when it stands on its legs, it's about as tall as a backpack you might carry to school.

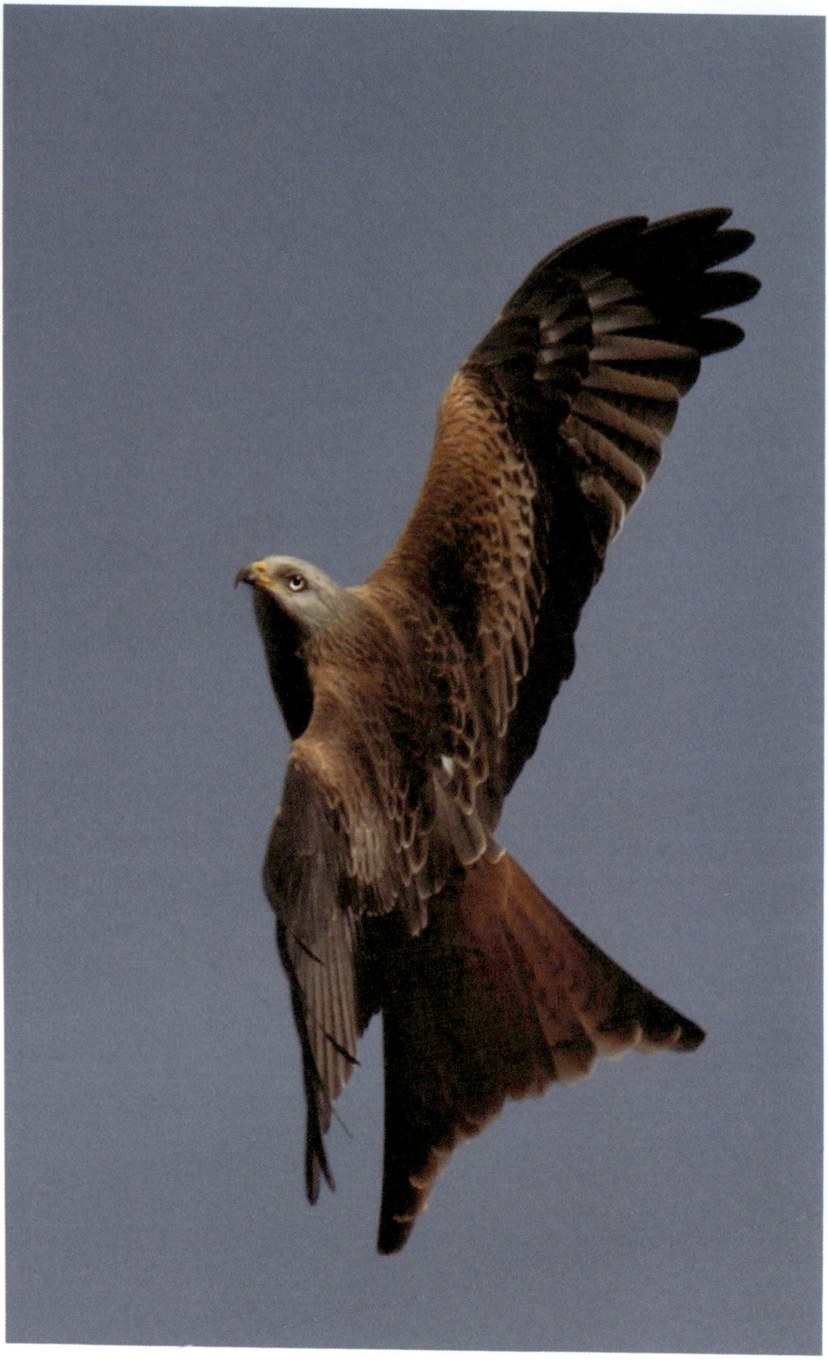

HABITAT

Red Kites are often seen soaring high in the sky above the countryside. They absolutely love wide open spaces! You can find them in places like farmlands, meadows, and even in the countryside near forests. They're not the kind of birds that like to live in big, noisy cities; they prefer quieter, peaceful areas.

One thing Red Kites really like in their habitat is trees. They use trees to build their nests and raise their little ones. So, you might see them near wooded areas or even in a big tree in your backyard if you're lucky!

These birds also enjoy living near rivers and streams. It's not just because they like the sound of flowing water; it's also because these watery places are great for finding food like fish and small creatures that live in the water.

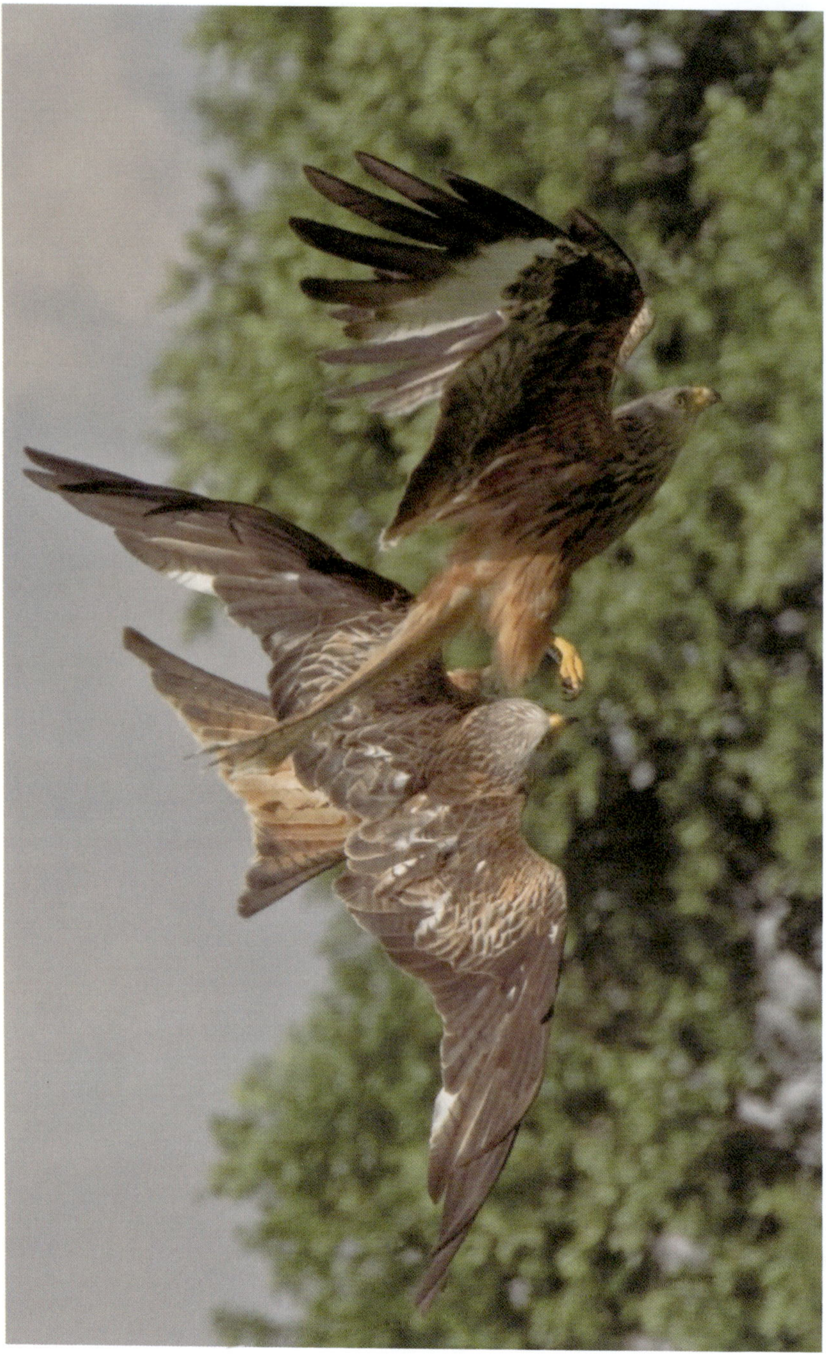

DIET

The Red Kite has a diet that's all about being a skilled hunter in the sky. These birds are carnivores, which means they like to eat meat instead of plants.

One of their favorite foods is small mammals. Imagine the Red Kite swooping down from the sky to catch things like mice, voles, and even young rabbits. They have sharp eyes that help them spot these little creatures from high above.

But that's not all they eat! Red Kites are also quite skilled at catching birds. They might snatch up smaller birds like sparrows or even grab a chick from a nest. It's like they have their very own birdy fast-food delivery service!

Sometimes, Red Kites go fishing. They'll fly over rivers and ponds, and when they see a fish swimming near the surface, they'll swoop down and grab it with their sharp talons.

These birds are known for being "opportunistic" eaters, which means they're pretty clever about finding food. If they see something tasty on the ground, like roadkill or scraps left behind by other animals, they won't say no to a free meal!

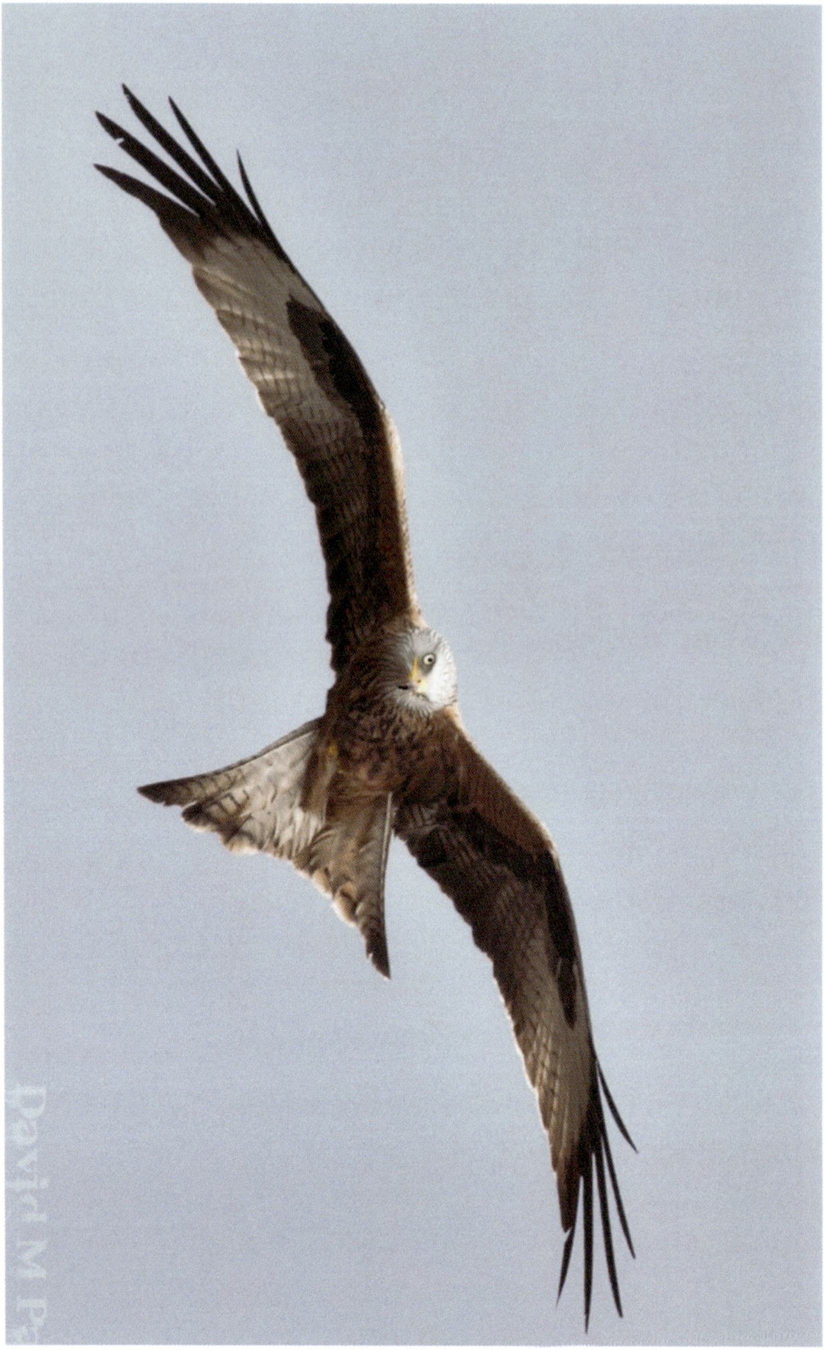

FRIENDS AND ENEMIES

The world of the Red Kite is filled with both friends and enemies.

Friends:

Other Red Kites: Red Kites are often seen flying and hunting together in groups. They are social birds and enjoy each other's company. You can think of them as feathered friends, helping each other find food and stay safe.

Crows and Ravens: Believe it or not, Red Kites sometimes team up with crows and ravens to find food. These birds are like their partners in crime when it comes to scavenging for meals.

Enemies:

Larger Birds of Prey: Red Kites have to be careful around bigger birds of prey like eagles and owls. These larger birds might see Red Kites as competition for food or even try to steal their meals.

Predators on the Ground: On the ground, Red Kite eggs and chicks can be at risk from animals like foxes, raccoons, and even other birds. That's why Red Kite parents work hard to protect their nests.

Cars and Power Lines: Red Kites sometimes face dangers from things like cars and power lines when they're flying low. These obstacles can be hazardous, and Red Kites need to watch out for them.

The Red Kites find strength in numbers when they're with their fellow Red Kites, but they also need to be on the lookout for potential dangers from other birds, animals, and traffic!

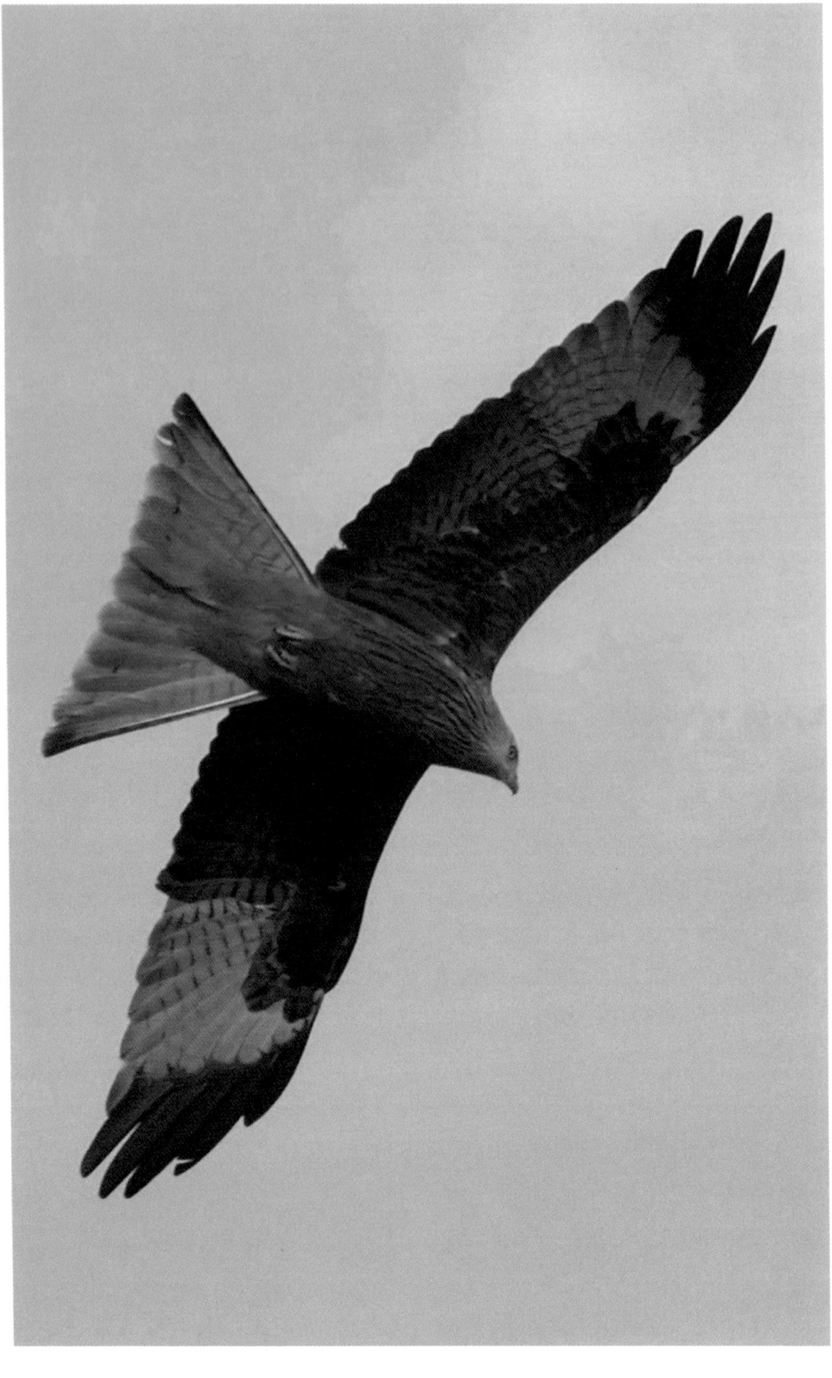

SUITABILITY AS PETS

Red Kites are not suitable as pets for many important reasons. These magnificent birds are wild and belong in the open skies and natural habitats, not in our homes.

Special Needs: Red Kites have unique needs that are hard to meet in a home setting. They need a lot of space to fly and exercise their strong wings. Keeping them in a cage would be like keeping a fish out of water; it's just not right for them.

Diet Challenges: Red Kites have specific diets that include hunting live prey. Providing the right food for them can be difficult and expensive. It's not like feeding a cat or a dog; it's more complicated.

Social Creatures: Red Kites are social birds and like to be with their own kind. They wouldn't be happy living alone in a cage or a house. It's essential for their well-being to have the freedom to soar and interact with other Red Kites.

Wild Spirit: These birds have a wild spirit and a strong instinct to be free. Trying to keep them as pets would be like trying to tame a wild animal, and it's not fair to them.

So, while Red Kites are amazing creatures to admire from a distance, they are not meant to be kept as pets. The best way to appreciate their beauty is by observing them in the wild or learning about them through books and documentaries.

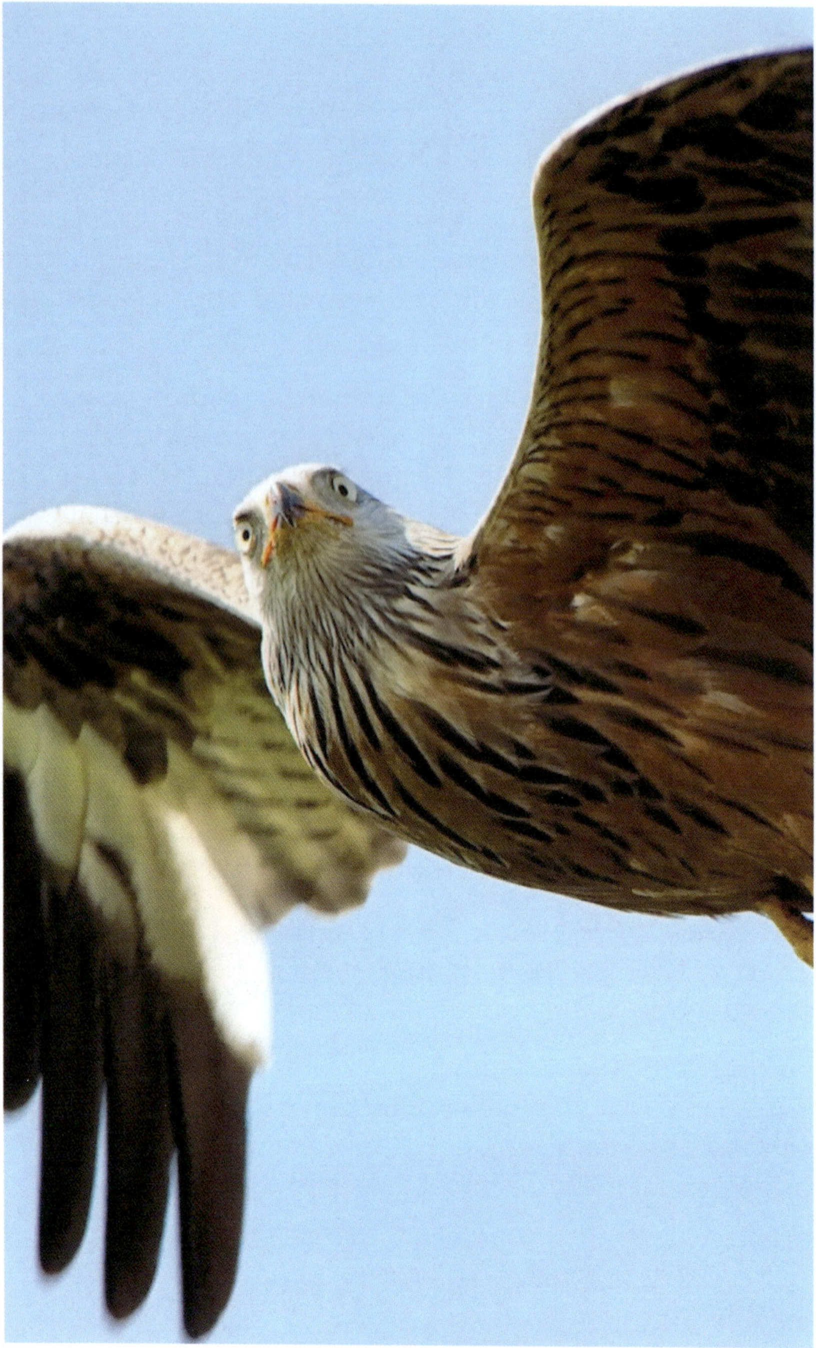

COLOR ME

COLOR ME

COLOR ME

COLOR ME

COLOR ME

COLOR ME

COLOR ME

COLOR ME

COLOR ME

COLOR ME

Please leave me a review here:

LisaStrattin.com/Review

For more Kindle Downloads Visit Lisa Strattin Author Page on Amazon Author Central

amazon.com/author/lisastrattin

To see upcoming titles, visit my website at LisaStrattin.com– most books available on Kindle!

LisaStrattin.com

FREE BOOK

FOR ALL SUBSCRIBERS – SIGN UP NOW

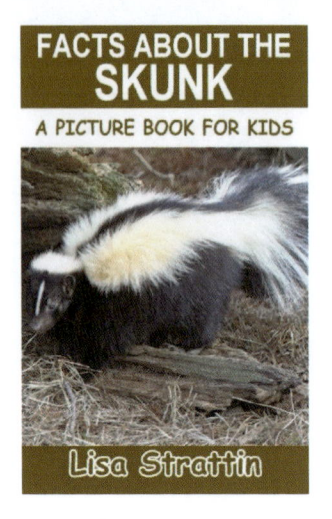

FACTS ABOUT THE SKUNK
A PICTURE BOOK FOR KIDS
Lisa Strattin

LisaStrattin.com/Subscribe-Here

LisaStrattin.com/Youtube